SandCastle™

Animal Sounds

Cats
Meow!

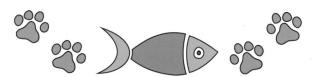

Pam Scheunemann

Consulting Editor, Diane Craig, M.A./Reading Specialist

ABDO
Publishing Company

Published by ABDO Publishing Company, 8000 West 78th Street, Edina, Minnesota 55439.

Editor: Katherine Hengel
Content Developer: Nancy Tuminelly
Cover and Interior Design and Production: Oona Gaarder-Juntti, Mighty Media
Photo Credits: Brand X Pictures, Digital Vision, ShutterStock

Library of Congress Cataloging-in-Publication Data
Scheunemann, Pam, 1955-
  Cats meow! / Pam Scheunemann.
    p. cm. -- (Animal sounds)
  ISBN 978-1-60453-568-6
  1. Cats--Juvenile literature. I. Title.
SF445.7.S33 2009
636.8--dc22
                              2008033918

SandCastle™ Level: Transitional

SandCastle™ books are created by a team of professional educators, reading specialists, and content developers around five essential components—phonemic awareness, phonics, vocabulary, text comprehension, and fluency—to assist young readers as they develop reading skills and strategies and increase their general knowledge. All books are written, reviewed, and leveled for guided reading, early reading intervention, and Accelerated Reader® programs for use in shared, guided, and independent reading and writing activities to support a balanced approach to literacy instruction. The SandCastle™ series has four levels that correspond to early literacy development. The levels are provided to help teachers and parents select appropriate books for young readers.

Emerging Readers **Beginning Readers** **Transitional Readers** **Fluent Readers**
(no flags)   (1 flag)   (2 flags)   (3 flags)

SandCastle™ would like to hear from you. Please send us your comments and suggestions.
sandcastle@abdopublishing.com

It is fun to have a cat as a pet.

Most cats do not like to get very wet.

When a cat is scared, it may make a hissing sound. This sound is a warning for everyone to keep away.

Cats will curl up and sleep all day.

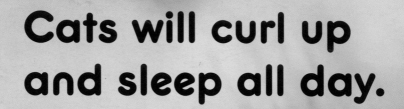

Cats purr when they are content. But they also may purr when they are hurt or sick.

But when they wake up, it's time to play.

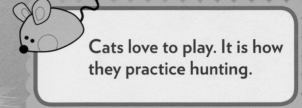

Cats love to play. It is how they practice hunting.

Many cats like to watch fish.

When cats are excited, they may make a chattering sound with their teeth.

This cat has a brand new dish!

Cats like to eat in quiet places. It is important to always put their food dishes in the same place.

Sometimes a cat will chase a mouse.

In the wild, cats hunt for their own food. When they chase mice and birds, they are using their hunting instincts.

I hope you don't have a mouse in your house!

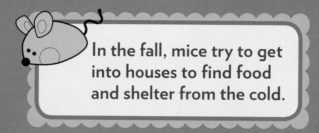

In the fall, mice try to get into houses to find food and shelter from the cold.

Cats have a very good sense of smell.

Like human fingerprints, no two cat noses are exactly the same.

They can sense things with their whiskers as well.

A cat's whiskers are very sensitive. They help cats feel their way around in the dark.

When a cat wants something right now, it lets you know with a big meow!

When cats meow they usually want to be fed, let outside, or given attention.

Glossary

chase (p. 14) – to run after someone or something in order to catch it.

content (p. 6) – happy and satisfied.

fingerprint (p. 18) – the mark made by the ridges in the skin on a fingertip.

hiss (p. 5) – to make a "ssss" sound like a snake when you do not like something.

imitate (p. 24) – to copy or mimic someone or something.

instinct (p. 14) – a natural pattern of behavior that a species is born with.

purr (p. 6) – to make a low, soft sound in the throat.

sensitive (p. 21) – able to sense the slightest change.

shelter (p. 17) – protection from the weather.

whisker (p. 21) – the long, stiff hairs that grow near an animal's mouth.

Animal Sounds Around the World

Cats sound the same no matter where they live. But the way that humans imitate them depends on what language they speak. Here are some examples of how people around the world make cat sounds:

English – meow   **French** – miaou
German – miau   **Greek** – miaou
Japanese – nyan, nyan   **Spanish** – miau

To see a complete list of SandCastle™ books and other nonfiction titles from ABDO Publishing Company, visit **www.abdopublishing.com**.

8000 West 78th Street, Edina, MN 55439 • 800-800-1312 • fax 952-831-1632